SOLACE & LIGHT

Fifty Trips Around the Sun

by Bob Christian

Edited by: Daisy Burton

ISBN: 9798326642851

©Bob Christian 2025

Disclaimer

The poetry anthology "Solace and Light" is a work of fiction. The characters, names, events, and incidents portrayed within this anthology are largely the product of the author's imagination. Any resemblance to real persons, living or dead, or actual events, is purely coincidental unless otherwise specifically stated.

The author is not responsible for any misinterpretation or offense caused by the content of this anthology. The poems included in this collection are artistic expressions, not meant to cause any offense, and should be viewed as such.

Readers are advised to approach this work with an open mind and understand that the themes, emotions, and experiences depicted are created for artistic purposes only.

Biography

This is a story of a young Bobbit and his adventures. Born in the rolling dales of Hoilant Ward Gate, he made a long journey with his two dragons (one with only one eye), to the shires of Narnia.

Bob was born the eldest son of a teacher and an engineer, in '70s Derbyshire. After a tough childhood and a stint in the Army, he followed in the footsteps of his grandad and became an engineer.

He had two beautiful daughters in quick succession in his early 20s, and they were his light and inspiration during some very dark times.

In 2012, he met the love of his life and moved to darkest Devon, where he married her and she became Mrs Bob. Not long afterwards, he received the diagnosis of Autism (Asperger's Syndrome at that time), having had various other, incorrect diagnoses previously. In 2017, he became a very proud grandad to his first granddaughter, and he now has four grandchildren.

He remains happily married to Mrs Bob, has a gorgeous rescue kitten, having recently lost another in tragic circumstances, and works in his dream job just a skip and hop from home.

Foreword

Hello … here we are again! I thought we'd said goodbye back in 2020 when I released what I thought would be my final book of poetry during the Covid-19 pandemic, but it seems I wasn't quite ready to stop scribbling.

Twenty years ago, I started therapy for serious depression, and what turned out to be a form of Autism, mixed with a dash of PTSD. Life was on the rocks. As I was struggling to process how I was feeling, it was suggested that I should write it down. I took an old A4 pad and started scribbling for hours in the dark; sometimes all night. Then, one day I realised that if you took some of what I'd written, cut some bits out and rearranged it, it resembled poetry.

My pieces started all those years ago, with scribbles like the loving verses of Angels, to the despair-ridden Cold Kiss of Steel. But over the years, although my style has changed and I have grown as a person, the passion and emotion behind what I write has always remained. Twenty years on, as I approach my fiftieth birthday, and six poetry books later, I have written fifty new pieces. I want to share them, so that you - my friends - can hopefully enjoy reading this chapter with me.

This poetry is not the only thing I've written: You can catch my musings and ramblings on my blog page, at: www.bob-christian.com

So let's get started. Please hold tight, and keep your arms inside the car at all times…

Dedication

This book is dedicated to the memory of Ollie. Not long on this earth, but a more heroic and loved cat has never existed.

Thank you for all you did for Noodles, for being a beautiful, loving cat for the short time we had you with us. I am so sorry that the world was so cruel to you.

Thank You....

Mrs Bob
I thank the universe every day that in this multiverse story, my 'me' met your 'you' and we became 'us'. You've stuck by me through thick and thin, and I could not have had the successful highs, or survived the lowest lows without you by my side. You are my wife, partner, lover, best friend, ultimate frustrater, and the proton to my neutron, endlessly spinning even after we leave this realm. I love you more than I ever thought possible.

J, R, & Big M
With heartfelt gratitude, love and sincere appreciation, I want to express my deepest thanks for your support, kindness and unwavering love and care. You have enriched my life in countless ways, most of which you probably have no idea about. Thank you for all you do.

Mentions

Henry
I can't remember a time when I didn't know you. You have always given sage advice, while keeping my latest sound-system-banger on the road. Most importantly, you were right by my side on that special December day in 2013.

Trouty
Welcome back, you tw@.

To You, The Reader
Thank you for taking time out of your day to read this or anything else I have written. I still find it strange that people want to read my scribbles, but I am eternally grateful that you do.

Table of Contents

No	Title
1	Foreword
2	Last Dance
3	Crafty
4	The Hive
5	Bedknobs
6	Counsel of Elders
7	L (Fifty)
8	Boxed Up
9	Probability Over X
10	Admission
11	PTSD
12	Auditor
13	Karma
14	Dear Young Me
15	Home Alone
16	Dog the Cat
17	The Journey
18	Witch Tryals
19	Handfast
20	Skjebne (Destiny)
21	Poetic Magick
22	iHuman v:50
23	Haunted
24	Broken Crayons
25	Renewal
26	Cold Kiss of Steel (The Final Cut)
27	Lian Yu
28	Shadow Boxing
29	Hero

30	The Feline Regime
31	Stacked
32	Old School
33	Lessons
34	Narnia (You chose wisely)
35	Grandad

36	The Bobbit (A Motorway Journey)
37	Summer Solstice
38	Winter Solstice
39	The Shire
40	Carnival of Souls
41	Dance of the Deities
42	Dreamworld
43	Unified Theory
44	Is This Your Card?
45	Dartington
46	Eights & Aces
47	Symphonies in the Royal Forest
48	Guardians
49	Farewell
50	Not All Heroes Wear Tuxedos

Foreword

Here we are again, back in this place.
I'm surprised and bewildered, with shock on my face.
I thought I was done, finished with this pen,
But I was wrong, it seems, once again.

I'll keep this foreword short - you've heard it all,
The ups and downs, with the rise and fall.
We're here for the poetry, that's the real deal,
To dive into emotions - to truly feel.

2020, a year of strangeness and strife,
Lockdowns and isolation were the rhythm of life.
Loneliness crept in, a companion unseen,
As I sat furloughed, chasing a dream.

I poured my thoughts into these written lines,
Clearing out my shed, as well as my mind.
These scribbles simply reflect my soul,
A departure from anger, a changing of role.

Proper poetry, I dared to proclaim!
A departure from the usual, a shift in my aim.
I hope you find solace, a connection that's deep,
In these words I've penned for you to keep.

But let me clarify, amidst all the ink,
Only a few pieces about family, I think.
Not about you, though this you may believe,
If it resonates with you it's a happy reprieve.

Beyond this book, there's more to explore,
Musings and ramblings, my world view galore.
On social media, my thoughts are shared,
Or my web page, where my stories are prepared.

Last Dance

On a beach where waves crash onto the shore,
An old man dances, his steps light and sure.
With the sun as his witness, the wind as his guide,
He twirls and he spins; he is lost in the tide.

Holding close in his arms his memories dear,
Of a love that once was, that's now absent yet clear.
The ethereal sense of his wife by his side,
They dance one more time now, their souls unified.

With each careful step, he recalls youthful grace,
And the echoes of laughter in his sacred space.
He feels sand through his toes - its soft embrace,
He moves to a rhythm he cannot erase.

Their shadows dance gently, entwined in the air,
Whispering words of true love beyond compare.
The waves play a symphony under the sun
As the man and his wife's forms just melt into one.

Time stands so still in this celestial dance,
The man finds such peace with this fleeting chance
To feel his wife's warmth, and her touch that's so real,
As they sway and they glide, in their eternal zeal.

With each gentle turn, he relives their deep bliss,
These chance stolen moments they'll forever miss.
But within this dance their true love is alive,
A testament, now, as the memories survive.

As the sun starts to set and it's painting the sky,
The old loving couple must now say goodbye.
But their dance will linger, forever embraced,
Forms etched on the beach never to be erased…

Crafty

In the shadow of the moon's soft glow,
Where whispers of enchantment flow,
A tale unfolds of mystic might,
In the realm of magic, dark as night.
Deep in a cauldron's bubbling brew,
Where secrets stir and mysteries stew,
Fingers graced by rings of silver hue,
Enchantments are woven; magic breaks through.

She dances with the spirits' grace,
A silhouette in moonlit space.
Her incantations fill the air,
Weaving spells with utmost care.
Her eyes, the windows to her soul,
Have ancient knowledge yet untold.
Her voice, a melody of power,
Echoes through the midnight hour.

She knows the herbs that heal and harm,
The chants that calm or raise alarm.
She treads the line of light and shade,
A sorceress in dark parade.
With broom in hand she takes to flight
Through starlit skies she soars with might.
Her destination's the hidden realm,
Where magical secrets can overwhelm.

In sacred circles, she casts her spell
With words that only witches tell.
Her craft a dance of fire and air,
Her casting skills beyond compare.
But do beware, oh mortal soul,
For witchcraft casts a heavy toll.
In realms of power tread with care,
And cast a spell – if you dare!

The Hive

In a world that's bursting with buzzing bee wonder
Lies the tale of a beekeeper, gentle and tender.
With a heart that's attuned to nature's deep song,
He attends to the hives where his little friends throng.

Veil and suit on, he'll approach their domain,
Respecting their kingdom, he's free from disdain.
Each hive is a treasure, a bustling community,
He listens to their humming, their pitch-perfect unity.

With smoke as his ally he calms down their wings,
Protecting their home and sweet honey it brings.
A dance of devotion, they whirl round and round.
The beekeeper's love for his hives is profound.

Through seasons of blooms their short journey unfolds,
From fragrant blossoms to jars of liquid gold.
He tends to them daily, their welfare's his creed,
He knows their survival is what we all need.

In their golden honey he finds a reflection
Of nature's own gift and the sweetest connection.
The man and his hives tells a tale so grand,
A testament to the delicate balance of this land.

With every jar filled, his gratitude rises,
For these pollinators are the world's silent prizes.
In the beekeeper's heart is a deep sense of pride,
He nurtures them still, man and bee side by side.

So, please, let us honour the beekeeper's plight,
And respect those bees, a magnificent sight.
For in their waggledance the secrets of life reside,
A glance at nature's beauty stretching far and wide.

Bedknobs

In a house enchanted, where love blooms,
Reside two witches with matching brooms.
A loving couple, their powers entwined,
Together they weave their spells undefined.

Existing with them are their kittens so fair,
Their eyes gleaming bright; mischief hangs in the air.
They prance and they play with a magical grace,
In this happy abode - their forever space.

The cauldron it simmers with potions galore,
Whispered incantations fill the air once more.
Chanting their spells they dance in delight,
They harness the moon under deep velvet night.

Walls are adorned with their herbs dried and rare,
Perfumes of enchantment they fill up their lair.
Books filled with knowledge both ancient and wise,
Unveiled secrets are drawn from the skies.

The hearth flickers gently with mystical flames,
Cast shadows that dance, yet they have no names.
Witches' laughs echo through cobwebby halls,
As they cast their spells within those sacred walls.

In this majick house love and power unite,
A haven of wonder where their dreams take flight.
With Ollie and Noodles, their kittens two,
The witches find solace in all that they do.

So let's celebrate this majick domain,
Where good spells are cast, and their wishes attained.
In this house of wonder enchantments reside.
May love, hope and majick always coincide.

Counsel of Elders

In a sunny market square they gather each week,
Some grumpy old men, all too weathered and wise.
With steaming coffee in hand they have a discussion,
Their voices carrying the weight of simpler times.

They reminisce together, lost in nostalgia
Of days when life moved at a gentler pace.
When the world seemed kinder; our hearts were lighter,
Before rushing and chaos were put in their place.

They speak of mornings spent in quietude,
Sipping hot brew in the warm morning sun,
Trading stories of youth with wrinkled smiles,
As the aroma of coffee blends with memories spun.

Their laughter mingles with the bustling square,
Echoing through the cobblestone streets,
And time will stand still for a brief moment there,
As they find joy in each other's feats.

They share tales of loves they have lost and have won,
Of battles they've fought and of dreams they pursued.
Though all their grumbles might seem bad-tempered,
Their hearts hold a warmth that can't be subdued.

In the company of their fellow old souls,
They find comfort in the shared camaraderie,
For in these brief moments of coffee and conversation,
They discover the essence of true harmony.

L
(Fifty)

Fifty. A number that holds significance and might,
A milestone reached; a journey in life's sight.
Let's explore the mathematical wonders it holds,
The facts about fifty, let's explore and unfold.

Fifty years, a span of time so fair,
Is eighteen thousand and fifty-six days' share.
That's 433,344 in hours,
A reminder of a number with mathematical powers.

Fifty. Divisible by one, two, five, ten,
A versatile number again and again.
Its factors are plenty, a mathematical array
Showing its flexibility in every way.

Fifty. The atomic number of tin,
A metal so useful, it's used both thick and thin.
Shown as an 'L' in numerals Roman,
A symbol of strength, and a bringer of omens.

Fifty. In geometry it appears as a pentagon,
A five-sided shape, a perfect polygon.
Each angle is one hundred and eight degrees,
A mathematical marvel, as I am sure you'll agree.

So, let's celebrate fifty, a number so grand,
With numerical facts that we now understand.
A milestone reached, a half-life well-lived,
A number that teaches, from which wisdom's derived.

Boxed Up

I fear my heart is cluttered up so
With memories held that I can't let go.
Each mistake, each wrong decision,
Engulfing me to the point of extinction.
They pile up in my mind like dusty relics
I want to forget – to stop feeling pathetic.
But the weight of my past is filling my mind
To the point where I simply cannot unwind.

Emotional pain slowly collects. I keep
It in hidden corners, all buried deep.
Clinging to the hurt like a prized possession,
Unable to find a healthy expression.
I stack my regrets like towering walls
Built high to shield from the pain I recall.
But those walls leave me trapped and confined,
Bound by the pain that I can't leave behind.

Now I'm a prisoner of my own design,
A hoarder of anguish, a collector of time.
Unable to free me, unable to heal,
I suffocate under the weight I conceal.
But it's time to release this burden I hold,
To free myself – now it's time to be bold.
In letting go lies the strength to get mended,
To break myself free from the walls that I've rendered.

I'll sort through the wreckage; discard what I must,
And make room for healing, for love and for trust.
No longer a hoarder of pain and regret,
I've learned to forgive. No more years of upset.
And in letting it go, I've now found my release,
I'm living in love, harmony and peace.
No longer pain-hoarding, but a soul setting free
To embrace the true beauty that my life can be.

Probability Over X

Buried in the vast realm of Twitter's endless chatter,
A serendipitous moment; a connection that mattered.
Amidst the noise and chaos a picture caught my eye,
String Theory for Dummies - I was so surprised.

In that simple image a door was unveiled,
To the depths of knowledge from where universes hail.
And in that one tweet a cosmic alignment occurred,
For in the multiverses, our souls finally stirred.

Across the expanse of timelines and space,
Our spirits intertwined in a celestial embrace.
Two souls seeking truth, traversing the unknown.
In the realm of ideas, seeds of love were sown.

With each reply, our minds started to dance,
Exploring the mysteries of this cosmic chance.
The symphony of our thoughts harmoniously blended.
As the universe conspired, our love was cemented

Through our conversation we shared our dreams,
In 280 characters we found infinite streams.
In the tapestry of tweets a love story unfurled,
Weaving together our souls in a parallel world.

From timelines to lifelines, our paths intertwined.
As we explored the depths of each other's minds.
Our tweets, emojis and hashtags expressed
The depth of our love and the bond we possessed.

So let's celebrate this love that was born on a screen,
For in the realm of Twitter our souls were seen.
String theory is complex, but our love is simple,
A connection that spans universes, it's truly eternal.

Admission

In the depths of despair, a battle you've fought alone,
Barely conscious, now, in a world that's unknown.
Lights flashing by, a blur of uncertainty,
In this chaotic moment you're seeking serenity.
Voices surround you, questions probing deep,
Their silent judgement's a wound that will weep.
Guilt and embarrassment weigh heavy on your heart,
In this fragile state you are wrecked; torn apart.

But know that you're never defined by this pain,
There is strength in you, ready to be regained.
For looking for help is a courageous endeavour,
To heal all your wounds - they won't haunt you forever.
In the halls of the hospital, a sanctuary of care,
A compassionate haven where burdens are shared.
Hands are extended with care so sincere,
They guide you to healing, erasing your fear.

For the darkness you faced and the battles you fought,
Speak volumes of resilience, it's a lesson well taught.
In the depths of despair hope can still reignite,
A flame of redemption burning always so bright.
Guilt and embarrassment won't define your birth,
For seeking help proves your strength and your worth.
Remember, too, you're not alone in this fight,
There are hands you can hold, they'll guide to the light.

For your emotional state does not define your fate,
Hold onto your hope, for it's never too late.
With love and support you'll find the strength to mend,
Rise from the ashes, let your spirit transcend.
Let the lights guide you through the darkest of nights,
Towards a new dawn where hope is your right.
Embrace the long journey, let the healing begin,
For in this raw state your new life will begin.

PTSD

In the depths of despair, in the shadows of the mind,
I found myself standing on the edge,
teetering
on the line.

The weight of the world pressing down,
suffocating
my soul,

The darkness consuming me, swallowing me
whole.

The whispers of doubt…   the screams of pain,
Battles raging within, driving me
INSANE.
Lost in a sea of emptiness, drowning in my fears,
The end seemed near –
I shed rivers of tears.

But in the darkness…
A flicker of light…
a glimmer of hope burning ever so bright.
I clench my fists, grit my teeth. I rise from the ashes,
I defy belief.
Surviving suicide, a warrior reborn.
From the depths of despair, a new day has dawned.
I stand tall, I stand strong… I am a survivor,
I belong.

To those who struggle, who feel lost in the storm,
Hold on tight – you WILL transform.
You ARE worthy, you ARE loved,
You are a fighter and you will rise above.

Auditor

In the depths of darkness, shadows dance and sway,
Death wanders his home, eternally astray.
Through dimly lit halls he roams with measured grace,
A collector of souls in his cold dwelling-space.

Rows of hourglasses standing tall and still,
Each one a testament to life's vibrant thrill.
They represent souls, their stories intertwined,
As Death, The Auditor, keeps your soul in mind.

With each step he takes, a hush falls in the air,
For Death is a presence that's feared but is fair.
He moves with great purpose; gaze steady and keen,
Weaves through corridors where darkness convenes.

In this realm of his, time's grasp starts to fade,
As Death judges the balance that each life has made.
He knows the weight of your soul, its joys and its woes,
A collector of memories as your life starts to close.

Silently he observes, his eyes hold the night,
For he is the keeper of life's final flight.
Though his presence may chill, his role is profound,
For Death brings closure - in peace he is found.

So don't fear his visit, but instead understand,
That Death's a collector with the gentlest hand.
In the darkened halls where hourglasses reside,
He gathers up souls as the sand subsides.

For in the tapestry of existence, Death plays his part,
An auditor of souls with a compassionate heart.
And as the sands of time continue to flow,
He reminds us of life's beauty, to cherish and know.

Karma

In the place where karma's whispers weave,
And witchcraft's powers begin to cleave,
A dance of forces in cosmic sway,
Where a witch and karma meet halfway.
My spells and potions I do prepare
To guide karma's path with the utmost care.
A nudge or a whisper - a touch so light,
In the kingdom of fate the touchpaper ignites.

For karma is a force that binds us all,
Responding to actions both great and small.
Yet, as a witch, I have the power
To guide its course through the darkest hour.
With intentions so pure and my heart straight-aligned,
I seek only to aid, not control or to bind.
A gentle encouragement, a nudging spell,
To ensure that justice is where it should dwell.

For karma's wheels turn with its own might,
But at times needs assistance to really shine bright.
I lend a hand with magic's embrace,
To steer it towards a just and fair place.
Through soft moonlit nights and whispered chants,
I weave all my spells, casting in advance.
With respect and reverence for the unseen,
I nudge karma, as a witch, and remain serene.

For in this realm where magic's entwined,
Karma and witchcraft are both aligned.
A symbiotic dance of power and grace,
Influencing destiny's sacred space.
So let us tread this path with respect,
Embracing karma's wisdom unchecked.
As a witch, I nudge with love and care,
Guiding karma, to ensure that justice is there.

Dear Young Me

As I sit here, reflecting on the journey I've travelled,
I write this letter for you to unravel.
In the concrete maze where despair seems to reign,
I urge you. Hold onto hope. Reach through your pain.

Take the time to savour those precious moments,
Embrace the laughter; joy; friendships so potent.
For in years to come these memories will be treasure,
A source of strength, a reminder of life's true measure.

Take time to heal the wounds that lie within,
To mend broken pieces, let rehab begin.
Keep moving forward, both physically and mentally,
In embracing your growth you'll find resilience eventually.

Take time out to create stories that will endure,
Ones that future generations will retell and ensure
That your legacy lives on; a flame that never dies,
In the hearts of your children, they'll reach for the skies.

Live for future generations, dear younger self,
Let your actions be a testament to love, courage, health.
Your past struggles have shaped you into who you are,
But the choices you make now will carry you far.

So, my dear younger self, heed my words with care,
Live your life with purpose and always be aware
The road may be tough, but you have strength within
To make a bright future, where new stories begin.

Home Alone

In a house that stands weathered and old,
A wizened man lives, his heart heavy and cold.
Surrounded by shadows, memories of the past,
The ghost of his wife, a true love that did last.

In every dark corner he can see her face,
Feel the touch of her hand; her warm embrace.
Her laughter still echoes through empty, dark hallways,
Yet her love still lingers, filling up his long days.

In the worn-out old armchair where he now sits alone,
He feels her presence like she'd never gone.
Photographs on the walls, frozen moments in time,
Each one a treasure; memories so sublime.

He walks through the rooms once filled with her light,
Her perfume still lingers: a fragrant delight.
The tunes that they loved still dance in the air,
A symphony of love, a bond beyond compare.

With each floorboard creak, he hears her voice
With warm words of comfort, she gives him a choice.
To stay where he is, hold her memory dear,
Or move on, let go - find new love somewhere near.

But he cannot do that, he can't let go of her!
Those things that remind him have such a strong lure.
He feels less alone with the memories remaining
Of his beautiful wife, they'll forever sustain him.

So, he sits in their house, which is weathered and old,
With the ghosts of his memories, the tales often told.
For love transcends time, and though no longer here,
Her spirit lives on; brings him solace and cheer.

Dog the Cat

In a cosy home where memories reside,
A couple bid farewell with tearful eyes,
To their dear feline friend, a one-eyed cat,
Who brought comfort and love in return for a pat.
With heaviest hearts, they must say their goodbyes,
But little do they know that fate has a surprise.
For through their door, with a crash and a thud,
Comes a black kitten, full of life and of love.

He bounds into their lives with a playful glee,
Bringing laughter and joy for all to see.
A mischievous spirit so full of zest,
He instantly becomes their most welcomed guest.
They call him "Dog" with a loving embrace,
For he plays fetch and goes for walks with grace.
A feline soul with a canine heart,
Weaves his way into the family - a most precious part.

With each passing day their bond grows so strong,
As Dog fills their home with a miaowing song.
He chases long shadows, dances in the sun,
Bringing laughter and happiness to everyone.
The couple find renewed youth and cheer
As they watch Dog play – he just has no fear!
He reminds them of the beauty in every day,
And teaches them to cherish moments along the way.

Though his time with them was a fleeting bliss,
And the love he brought they'll forever miss.
In those few short years, their hearts were touched
By a playful black kitten who loved so much.
When the day came to say goodbye,
They held him close and softly cried.
With memories etched deep in their souls,
They'll cherish the love that he helped to unfold.

The Journey

In a world of shadows where hope seemed thin,
Two kittens wandered, their journey to begin.
Abandoned and alone with no place to rest,
They longed for a home with love that's blessed.
Through tangled forests on moonlit trails
They searched for warmth, their little hearts frail.
But fate had a plan, a twist in their quest,
For they stumbled upon a home quite unlike the rest.

A cottage nestled deep in the woods,
Where magic danced and potions brewed.
A couple, enchanting and wise, lived inside,
Witches by nature, using love as their guide.
With gentle hands and hearts so kind,
They welcomed the kittens, what a treasure to find!
With a wand's gentle touch and a low-whispered spell,
The kittens knew instantly that all would be well.

In this mystical abode, they found their place,
With cauldrons a-bubble and spells to embrace.
The witches' love, like a warm, healing light,
Banished their fears and made safe the night.
Named Luna and Stardust, a celestial pair,
With playful antics and fur oh so fair.
They'd curl up on broomsticks and join in the flight,
As they soared high under the moon's gentle light.

In this magical home, they were cherished - adored,
With cuddles and purrs, their spirits soared.
The witches' love and magic, a bond unbreakable,
Their hearts intertwined, forever unshakable.
So, the abandoned kittens found their bliss,
In a home of wonder, with nothing amiss.
From darkness to light, their journey's complete,
With the witches as family - life's sweetest of treats.

Witch Tryals

In the shadows they dwelt, both wise and kind,
Witches with knowledge, a gift to mankind.
But fear and ignorance swept through the land,
Persecution and prejudice they could not withstand.

For their healing herbs and scientific ways,
Deemed as witchcraft, were met with a fiery blaze.
Accused of sorcery with no evidence clear,
Their wisdom and compassion replaced by fear.

But through the darkness their legacy remains,
Their wisdom and teachings all fully retained.
For witches were guardians of nature's grace,
Their murders a stain that should not be erased.

Let us remember their courage, their plight,
And honour their memory with love and with light.
For all those unjustly accused in the past,
Will forever inspire and their wisdom will last.

Handfast

In this sacred moment, two souls unite,
Their love like a flame burning always so bright.
With vows whispered softly and promises made,
A journey embarked on, this love will never fade.

Like leaves on a tree their love will grow,
Stronger with each passing day, a steady flow.
Breath by breath their bond will get stronger,
All strife and problems I know that they'll conquer.

Please bless this couple with love that's pure,
May their hearts be steadfast and their love endure.
As we tend to all things on this earthly plane,
May they tend to their love, and dance again.

With nurturing care and patience, they'll sow
Seeds of affection that will continue to grow.
For love, like a garden, requires tender heed,
Watered by respect it will surely succeed.

May their love be a beacon guiding their way,
Through each season of life, come what may.
Together, they'll face life's trials and tests,
With unwavering love, they'll give of their best.

So let us celebrate this union divine,
Two hearts entwined, their love will shine.
With vows spoken true, their destiny sealed,
In eternal love, forever revealed.

Skjebne
(Destiny)

In the ancient inspiring land of Norse,
With myth and legend at its source,
Stood proud their mighty runestones
Carved with symbols; ancient tomes.

Upon those stones are stories told
Of heroes brave and battles bold.
The runes etched deep with secret might,
Guiding souls through day and night.

This glimpse of history will last,
Each stone's a portal to the past.
They speak of gods and cosmic lore,
Of Odin's wisdom; Thor's call to war.

Elder Futhark, the sacred code,
Guiding warriors on their road
Through forests dark and oceans wide,
Rune stones stood as a warrior's guide.

From Jelling through to Gotland's shore,
Rune stones stand forever more.
Guarding the tales of warriors bold,
Their legacy etched in stone, now told.

So let us honour the ancient stones,
Those Norse runes, their power well-known.
For in their presence we find our way,
Connecting us to yesterday.

Poetic Magick

In a realm where words dance and dreams take flight,
A poet's pen holds power, shining so bright.
With ink and parchment, spells are spun,
Changing poetry to magic – it's easily done.

Like a witch, casting spells under the moon's gaze,
The poet weaves enchantment in myriad ways.
Each line a spark of crackling energy
Igniting souls, and setting hearts free.

Through the rhythm and rhyme a spell is cast.
Words woven together; a tapestry vast.
Within every stanza, a flicker of flame
Is guided by the poet's mystical aim.

The power of language, a potent brew
Is infused with magic, both old and new.
Verses become charms when spoken with intent,
Unleashing forces that Christians lament.

Fireballs from fingertips as poetry unfolds,
Empowering the writer as the story is told.
The pen becomes a wand, casting its spell,
Transforming reality into a land where dreams dwell.

So simple yet majestic, this alchemy of words,
A poet's incantation, where magic is heard.
In the realm where poetry and spells entwine
The poet's power is a force divine.

iHuman v:50

In a world of ones and zeros we dwell,
iHuman50 is our digital shell.
Through screens and pixels our lives unfold,
Entangled in social media's hold.

A virtual world where connections are made,
But are they real or just a charade?
Likes and comments, a currency of worth,
We chase validation on this digital earth.

Scrolling through feeds, lost in the abyss,
Seeking validation, searching for bliss.
Snapshots of happiness so carefully curated,
But behind the filters, our soul's suffocated.

iHuman50, an upgrade's been won,
Yet our hearts grow colder, empathy gone.
As we stare into screens, losing touch with reality,
Our lives fragmented - a shattering duality.

Loneliness lingers in this digital age,
As human connection becomes a mirage.
We're wired, connected, but feel so alone,
Lost in a sea of faces held on a 'phone.

So let us unplug and break free from this haze.
Rediscover the human connection's embrace.
For in the offline world true connections reside,
Where empathy, compassion and love coincide.

Let's find our humanity, our essence so true,
Find comfort in the warmth of hearts that beat through.
iHuman50, find us the balance we crave,
And reclaim our lives from this digital grave.

Haunted

In these lonely halls, I wander aimlessly,
Forever chasing echoes of what used to be.
Ghostly memories, fleeting and bittersweet,
Reminding of the times our hearts would meet.

Since the day I lost you, I search for solace,
Longing for the company, the love we possessed.
You were my best friend, my companion - in you,
I found my multiverse, my world anew.

But now, a once-warm home lays desolate.
Reduced to a place of emptiness and fate.
A cold, darkened mausoleum, devoid of light,
Where shadows haunt the endless night.

Yet, in my heart, your spirit still lives,
Guiding me through the darkness where hope exists.
Though you are now gone, your love forever stays,
Through my memories, there's peace in the maze.

So I'll keep wandering, searching for a trace,
Clinging to memories of the love we embraced.
For in this cold and lonely place,
I'll wait for the moment I see your face.

Broken Crayons

Within this darkness, where shadows lay,
A story unfolds in shades of grey.
Broken crayons, once vibrant and bold,
Now carry the scars of stories untold.
PTSD survivors, warriors so strong,
Facing their personal terrors so long.
Torn fragments of memories, haunting and grim,
Yet within is a spirit that never dims.

Like broken crayons they still hold the power
To colour the world in each passing hour.
Though broken, their colours shine so bright,
Guiding others through the darkest nights.
With empathy and strength they lend a hand,
Hiding the battles they always withstand.
Each stroke on canvas is a tale of survival,
A testament to their gradual revival.

So please acknowledge their strength and their grace,
And hold them close in a warm embrace.
For broken crayons still hold the key
To a world where healing sets us free.
I hope their journey finds comfort and peace,
And that their colours will never cease.
For in their fragments a masterpiece is found,
PTSD survivors, in trauma bound.

Renewal

Each night, he wakes up screaming in despair,
In a puddle of sweat, barely aware.
Nightmares fill his head. The relentless voice
Repeating his torment, it gives him no choice.

Like a record stuck on repeat, it plays its tune,
Terrifying him, he's left marooned.
He fears the solitude, the darkness of the night,
But he'll feel stronger in the morning light.

As he awakens from his troubled sleep,
His sanity he'll strive to keep.
For the shadows of the night still linger,
But he grasps the hope - a tiny glimmer.

Each breath he takes is a step towards healing,
A chance to find peace and a new beginning.
No longer drowning in the past's cruel tide,
He'll conquer his fears; let his spirit guide.

Though the fear may persist, haunting his mind,
He'll silence its echoes, and leave them behind.
With love - self-compassion - he'll find his way,
No longer held captive by the night's disarray.

For he's not alone in this battle he faces,
In the arms of his love he'll find his grace.
Together they'll stand - face the darkest night
And find solace in love that shines so bright.

Cold Kiss of Steel
(The Final Cut)

From depths of despair, he seeks release,
Lost in the labyrinth of his own pain.
He turns to music in a desperate attempt
To express those feelings he struggles to explain.

Embracing the darkness that engulfs him,
Preparing for a battle with unseen foes.
Agony surrounds him from every angle,
A relentless torment that never slows.

Losing control, emotions run wild,
Like a tempest that ravages his mind.
In this chaos there is a strange relief
In the gentle kiss of steel enshrined.

It brings a balance to the turmoil,
A temporary release from life's cruel ride.
But as the light pierces the darkness,
He spies the demons the shadows hide.

They retreat, banished by the blinding light,
Like a nightmare fading with the dawn.
Yet he wakes to the harsh reality before him,
Scars etched deep, the blood's been drawn.

That kiss, a sensation that can't be described,
A momentary relief, kind and complete.
But the scars remain, unlike fleeting memories,
A reminder of battles he's had to meet.

Let's break the silence that shrouds this pain,
Seek understanding, compassion, and care.
For in unity, we can find strength to heal,
And offer a hand to the souls being bared.

Lian Yu

In a world of grey where time stands still,
I navigate through life, devoid of thrill.
Each day a repetition, an endless loop
A soul so weary my mind's like soup.
Home is my sanctuary, so I'm led to believe
But wearing death's cloak makes me want to leave.

Alone in my house, in the silence I creep,
Thoughts of escape are a secret I keep.
In the depths of despair I contemplate
An end to this existence, to seal my own fate.
But little do I know that I'm already gone
A ghost in a shell, an existence withdrawn.

Weeks turn to months, and time slips away.
I'm stuck in purgatory, an unknowing stay.
No more can I yearn, no more can I dream.
In this twisted reality forever, it seems.
A life so mundane a soul left undone
In my purgatory alone – I'm left with no one.

Shadow Boxing

In the depths of a wounded soul, a battle fiercely rages,
A silent war, fought within, through life's relentless stages.
PTSD, a haunting spectre, its grip so tight and strong,
In a cold society that says, "*Man up, move along.*"
Each day begins with courage, a hesitant step forward.
But the weight of the memories can't be ignored.
Past echoes linger, haunting every thought,
As society scorns, "*Hide the battles that you've fought.*"

In his reflection, a warrior stands alone.
A mask of bravery, a face that's not his own.
The world demands a stoic front, a facade tough and cold.
Inside, a storm of emotions - a story yet untold.
The wounds of war invisible, but etched upon the soul,
Constant reminders of the battles that took a heavy toll.
Triggers lurk in shadows waiting to unleash their might,
Society shouts louder, "*Don't show weakness – fight!*"

But strength is not in silence, in suppressing pain untold.
It's in the courage to seek help; to let healing unfold.
For warriors are not defined by the battles they have faced,
But by their resilience and bravery; their ability to embrace.
So let us break the chains of stigma, the notion to '*man up,*'
Create more understanding, instead of just '*cheer up*'.
For in the battle with trauma, no one should fight alone,
In a society that truly cares, compassion should be shown.

Let's listen to the whispers of those who bear the weight,
Build a foundation of support where help's never too late.
For the strength to face each day, overcome the darkest night,
Is found in bonds of brotherhood, love's unwavering light.
So let us stand together, with our hearts entwined,
Supporting one another, in a world that's truly kind.
Their battles and their awful pain, with support might fade,
In a society that understands it's okay to be afraid.

Hero

In the realm of parenthood is a bond so true,
A correlation between your idol and you.
For in your child's eyes you're a figure so bold,
A comic book hero with strength untold.

With a heart full of love you soar through their dreams,
Guiding them through all life's turbulent streams.
You're their Superman, their monster detector,
A symbol of hope, their ultimate protector.

Just like Batman, you fight off their fears,
Keeping them safe, wiping away their tears.
You're their Dark Knight - in the shadows you stand,
Guarding their innocence with an unwavering hand.

As Spider-Man, you teach them to be brave.
To face challenges head-on, and never to cave.
You're their friendly neighbourhood hero, you see,
Inspiring them to be the best they can be.

Wonder Woman's spirit resides in your heart,
Empowering your child as wisdom you impart.
Their Amazonian warrior, fierce and strong,
Teaching them resilience when things go wrong.

The Flash you embody with lightning speed,
Making time for them, fulfilling every need.
You're their superhero, always there in a crisis,
A constant presence, and as strong as Colossus.

In the world of parenthood, you wear the cape,
Embracing the role, always there in a scrape.
For comic book heroes may captivate their view,
But the greatest hero, dear parent, is you.

The Feline Regime

Open the door, and BOOM!
The world outside vanishes like last week's leftovers,
Flying away like a bad date you keep ghosting.
Two pairs of eyes, glowing like tiny traffic lights,
Pierce through the dimness,
Saying, *"Oh good, you're back!*
We've only waited a millennium!"
Soft bodies crash into my legs like
Fur-covered freight trains,
The ultimate greeting party.
Not here for snuggles, no,
But to audition for the role of Obstacle In My Path.
Their paws are relentless messengers,
Tapping out urgent Morse code:
"Feed us, human! And while you're at it,
bow down to our furry greatness!"

Here I am, back at home sweet home,
Where my job is clear;
I'm the butler in this kitty kingdom.
They're the royalty, plotting to conquer the world
One hairball rebellion at a time.
Ollie and Noodles, my pint-sized tyrants,
Whose sole mission is to nap on every available surface,
Except, of course, the plush throne I bought them,
Which sits untouched, pristine as a museum exhibit.
I flop onto the couch and they follow like
Shadows with an agenda,
Determined to suffocate me with love,
And a hint of fishy breath.

Cont'd

The Feline Regime
(Cont'd)

Their antics are a sitcom I never subscribed to,
But here we are,
In the never-ending season of
"*Two Cats and One Worn-Out Human.*"
Somehow, their chaos is the highlight of my day.
In their eyes, I see the reflection of every
Cat meme ever shared,
And I realise, with a chuckle that
I'm not just a mere mortal in their eyes,
But their favourite show, streaming live,
24/7, no ads, no breaks.
So here I am, the proud servant of Ollie and Noodles,
The tiny overlords of my heart and my home.
And as I sit, covered in fur with a dignity
that's long since fled,
I think life is pretty great because
Nothing says "*Welcome home*"
Like a purring plot to rule the universe,
One treat at a time.

Stacked

Once upon a time, in a little old town,
Lived a grandad with a smile both happy and warm.
Every day he set off on a grand adventure,
Walking miles and looking for a pasty to capture.
With his hat on his head, walking stick in his hand,
He'd shuffle along, exploring each nook and strand.
Through winding streets a path he'd beat,
Searching high and low to find his tasty treat.

With each step he took, he'd reminisce and recall,
The pasties he'd loved, each one and all.
Remembering the flaky crust and the savoury filling,
His mouth would water, his anticipation thrilling.
He'd visit bakeries and cafes, asking for a pasty,
But they said, "*Sorry, no, but our cakes are so tasty!*"
Undeterred, he pressed on, determination unwavering,
He knew that soon a delight he'd be savouring.

One cold day, as he walked, feeling quite frozen,
He saw a shop with a sign, "*Pasties – we're open!*"
His heart skipped a beat, as he entered with glee,
Could this be the place where his pasty would be?
The aroma of fresh-baked pastry filled the air,
The sight of golden crusts made him stop and stare.
He ordered one, with a twinkle in his eye,
And as he took a bite, with joy he sighed.

The pasty was perfection, just as he had dreamed,
The flavours danced on his tongue, or so it seemed.
With a smile on his face he said his goodbyes,
And with newfound zeal he carried home his prize.
From that day on he took a new route,
Each morning he'd walk to the shop for his loot.
For he had found treasure, those pasties divine,
And he savoured each bite every time.

Old School

In the hallowed corridors of a boarding school's embrace,
Where dreams take flight in infinite space,
A group of kindred souls bound by passions so rare,
With comic books, roleplay, and battles to share.

In hidden corners and nooks their haven they find,
Immersed in their heroes, their minds all intertwined.
Portals to realms that are adventure bound,
Where masked crusaders and villains are found.

With capes fluttering and powers unleashed
They soar through panels, their imagination increased.
From Gotham's shadows to Asgard's halls,
Readers find shelter within ink-filled walls.

But beyond the pages quests still await,
In dungeons deep, where heroes meet their fate.
With dice in hand they weave tales profound,
As the Dungeon Master's voice echoes all around.

Warhammer fighters, all crafted with care,
Painted with precision, a love that they shared.
Brushstrokes brought life to warriors bold,
As they stood tall, stories waiting to be told.

Lessons

In the twilight of life, where wisdom's been won,
A story unfolds of a journey near-done.
The old and the wise, the silver of hair
Carry the scars of mistakes, it's the burden they bear.

For in the voyage of life, we stumble and fall,
Tripping on errors both big and small.
But the beauty of age lies in what we have gained,
The wisdom that blossoms from lessons ingrained.

With each misstep taken's a new understanding,
A map of experience, a guide for withstanding.
The old souls have weathered the storms of their past,
Learning from mistakes and ensuring they last.

They've tasted the bitterness of regret's embrace,
But emerged stronger, their mistakes have been faced.
They've stumbled and faltered but never stayed down,
For in every blunder seeds of wisdom are found.

They've learned the value of patience and time,
To navigate obstacles, to find peace sublime.
They've gained empathy borne from their pain,
And know that their errors were not made in vain.

Narnia *"You chose wisely"*

In the heart of Devon, a county so fair,
Is Totnes, a place of stories to share.
With its ancient streets, winding and steep,
A tapestry of history is woven deep.
The River Dart gives a tranquil embrace;
Inviting wanderers to find shelter and peace.
Boats gently glide on its shimmering tide,
A sanctuary of calm where dreams reside.

Nestled by the river's gentle flow,
It exudes a charm - it seems to glow.
With its colourful houses, painted and bright,
A kaleidoscope of beauty; a vibrant sight.
There's Totnes Castle standing tall and proud,
Guarding the town with a regal shroud.
Whispering tales of battles fought long ago,
Echoes of knights and kings lost in time's flow.

The bustling market's a lively affair,
Filled with aromas and food everywhere.
Local artisans, their crafts on display,
A haven for shoppers on any given day.
Totnesians form a community diverse,
Embracing change with a spirit immersed
In alternative lifestyles and eco-friendly ways,
Totnes leads the way with its forward gaze.

The town's a haven for free-spirited souls,
Where creativity and imagination have lead roles.
With an independent spirit, unconventional and bold,
It's a place where uniqueness unfolds.
So let us celebrate Totnes, this gem so rare,
A town with a heartbeat beyond compare.
With its rich heritage and a sense of pride,
In our hearts it will always reside.

Grandad

In the corner of the garden, where shadows gently fall,
An old wooden shed, weathered and worn stands tall.
A sanctuary of solitude where memories reside,
An old man finds contentment, his pipe by his side.

With each puff of smoke, he reminisces about the past,
Of days long gone by, too fleeting, too fast.
Hands, weathered and worn, create with tender care,
As he potters about, lost in his memories there.

In the shed's embrace, time seems to stand still,
He finds comfort in the silence; he is fulfilled.
With each stroke of paint and each nail that he drives,
He's happy in his shed; his spirit thrives.

The wood scent lingers - a familiar old friend,
As he ponders his life from beginning to end.
The pipe's gentle ember glows in the twilight's gleam,
A companion in solitude - this poet's dream.

The Bobbit
(A Motorway Journey)

In a bustling city where magic was rare,
Lived a witch with an eclectic flair.
With his vibrant robes and his staff of oak,
He set off on a journey, leaving the smoke.
Through the crowded streets he weaved his way,
Dreaming of the rolling hills where he'd stay.
In his heart was a longing for a much simpler life,
Away from the chaos; away from the strife.

He ventured forth, seeking the Shire's embrace,
A land that's untouched by the modern world's pace.
With each step he took, the city's noise grew faint,
As he entered a realm of magic so quaint.
In the Shire, he found a cottage so fair,
A haven of peace with love in the air.
His wife, a kindred spirit, with eyes so bright,
They embraced the enchantment, both day and night.

Ollie and Noodles, their feline companions,
Brought joy and games like mischievous dragons.
Their paws so nimble and their hearts so wild
Added warmth to the cottage; the couple beguiled.
Inland, by the Dart, where time seemed to pause,
He practiced his craft, obeying nature's laws.
Brewing potions with herbs from the garden's delight,
Spells whispered softly under the moon's pale light.

Friends sought his wisdom; his magical might,
For he brought healing, hope and insight.
With each incantation, the Shire would thrive,
The eclectic witch helped keep its spirit alive.
In the rolling hills, he found his true home,
A place where his spirit could freely roam.
The Lord of the Rings had nothing on this tale,
Of a witch's journey, so love could prevail.

Summer Solstice

On the longest day, when the sun stands high,
It's the summer solstice in the vast blue sky.
A time of celebration of warmth and light,
As nature's beauty shines so bright.

The earth, ablaze with golden rays,
Awakens dreams in a sunlit haze.
Fields of flowers dance in the breeze,
Their vibrant colours a sight to please.

The sun lingers, refusing to set,
Painting the horizon with hues of red.
The world comes alive in a joyful symphony,
As creatures revel in nature's harmony.

From dawn to dusk, the hours stretch long,
Inviting us to sing summer's sweet song.
With bare feet on warm sand and cool grass,
We embrace the season, letting time pass.

Bonfires crackle, illuminating the night,
As we gather around, our hearts burning bright.
Stories whispered and laughter in the air,
Under the solstice sky we have no cares.

For on this day, we celebrate the sun,
A reminder that life's cycles continue to run.
The summer solstice is a moment sublime,
A celebration of nature's grand design.

Winter Solstice

During the stillness of the longest night,
The world holds its breath, bathed in moonlight.
As winter's embrace tightens its grip,
The solstice arrives on its celestial trip.

The sun's heat now a distant memory,
It casts a pale glow with its wintry energy.
Silent whispers of frost adorn the land,
A frozen tapestry crafted by nature's hand.

The air is crisp; a symphony of cold;
Each breath a reminder of stories untold.
Beneath the starlit sky a blanket of snow,
A shimmering veil where secrets can grow.

The solstice marks a turning point,
A shift in the balance, a cosmic joint.
From darkness to light, the cycle starts,
Hope is reborn as new year does its part.

In the depths of the night a fire burns,
A beacon of warmth as the world slowly turns.
For in this moment we find depth and unity,
Bound by the solstice's ancient beauty.

So let us rejoice on this sacred night,
As we honour the darkness and welcome the light.
Winter solstice, a time to reflect and renew,
A reminder of life's cycles, both the old and the new.

The Shire

In a cottage nestled in the middle shires,
A lovely old couple sit warm by the fire.
With hearts entwined they share their days,
Their world untouched by time's relentless ways.

In their abode, humble and quaint,
A treasure trove of history's painted.
Antique furniture, each piece with a tale,
Whispered secrets of love's long trail.

A cat named Moz, with fur so fine,
Curled up in slumber, he's a snoring feline.
Content and cosy, by the hearth he lays,
Dreaming of adventures in fields far away.

Outside their cottage is a vibrant scene,
A family of wild pheasants, regal and serene.
Their feathers ablaze with colours so bright,
Dancing and fluttering in golden light.

Amid the pheasants a kite takes flight,
A bird of prey, an embodiment of might.
Eyes razor sharp and wings spread wide,
It soars through the air in a majestic glide.

With stories shared and memories made,
The old couple's love would never fade.
Their cottage is filled with treasures so old,
A testament to a life well-lived, we're told.

Within this sanctuary of affection and charm,
Lived the old couple; hearts locked; arm in arm.
With each tender touch their spirits elated,
In their quaint shire cottage their love's unabated.

Carnival of Souls

In a fairground of the mind, shadows play,
Where mental health's attractions bray.
A rollercoaster wild and free,
Climbs to a peak, then dives to the sea.
High above on a slender wire,
A balancing act above a fire.
Teetering emotions, left then right,
One step wrong and the world's alight.

Haunted houses, dark and deep,
Where secrets in the cupboards sleep.
Skeletons rattle, whispers low,
In corners where the dark winds blow.
The mirror maze reflects our fears,
Distorted truths; silent-shed tears.
Lost within, searching for the way,
Through winding paths of night and day.

Merry-go-rounds of endless thought,
Spin in circles with battles fought.
Laughter echoes then fades to grey,
As horses ride the dreams away.
In bumper cars we shout and clash,
Emotions strike and then we crash.
Bruises hidden, pain's concealed,
In a dance where nothing's ever healed.

The fairground lights they flicker bright,
Yet shadows linger out of sight.
In every ride a story's told,
Of hearts that break and minds that fold.
So step right up, the fair's in town,
Where pain and sorrow wear the crown.
In the carnival of the soul
We play our part, we seek control.

Dance of the Deities

Where hope and magic intertwine,
Where the love of god and goddess aligns,
There lays a tale of nature's embrace,
Of lunar cycles; animals; magical grace.
The god, a beacon of strength and might,
With sun-kissed hair and eyes so bright.
He roams the earth with a loving hand,
Protector of creatures across the land.

In forests deep, where animals reside,
He walks among them, side by side,
From majestic lions to gentle deer,
His presence brings calmness, void of fear.
The goddess, adorned with lunar glow,
Her hair cascades like moonlit snow,
She dances with tides in a rhythmic trance,
Weaving lunar cycles with celestial dance.

In twilight's hour, as day turns to night,
She calls upon creatures in gentle flight,
Owls hoot their wisdom, wolves howl their song,
As the goddess guides them all night long.
Together, god and goddess unite
In nature's embrace, their love takes flight,
They honour the cycles, both bright and dark,
Embracing the essence of life's sacred arc.

Cont'd

Dance of the Deities
(cont'd)

The god with his strength will always aid,
Protect and nurture amidst the glade,
While the goddess with her lunar sway,
Brings harmony and balance, night and day.
Magical energies course through their veins,
As they weave spells, releasing our chains.
They channel the power of earth and of sky,
Creating wonders that never shall die.

In their union, nature finds its voice,
As they honour the creatures and rejoice.
For the god and goddess, in love do dwell,
Creating a world where magic excels.
So let us celebrate this divine pair,
Their relationship with nature's beyond compare,
May we embrace their teachings and their ways,
And honour their presence throughout our days.

Dreamworld

In a land of darkness where shadows loomed,
A princess stood tall in a world of gloom.
Battling demons, her spirit fierce and bright,
She fought with courage in the dead of night.

Her heart was burdened, her soul was torn,
But she never gave up, nor was she forlorn.
With sword in hand and armour gleaming,
She faced the darkness, her spirit beaming.

Through desolate landscapes she journeyed on,
Searching for hope til the break of dawn.
Her footsteps echoed in silent despair,
But she pushed forward with unwavering care.

The demons screeched, their voices so loud,
Trying to break her, to make her feel cowed.
But she found strength deep down in her core,
To face the darkness; to fight; to restore.

With each battle won her resolve grew stronger,
She knew in her heart that she could not linger.
She yearned for freedom, for a world of light,
To banish the darkness, to end the fight.

Cont'd

Dreamworld
(Cont'd)

And then, at last, the truth was revealed,
In a moment of clarity her fate unsealed.
She woke from her slumber, her eyes open wide,
Discovering she had been lost in a dream inside.

In a coma she'd dwelt trapped in her mind,
A world of despair, with hope hard to find.
But through her journey, she learned to believe
That even in darkness, a light she could see.

With newfound strength, she faced her reality,
Embracing life's challenges with vitality.
A princess no longer trapped in a dream,
She conquered her demons with a triumphant gleam.

So let her story be a reminder to all,
That even in darkness, we can stand tall.
For within ourselves, the power resides,
To overcome struggles and let hope guide.

Unified Theory

In this tapestry of time, my love, I must confess,
I've stumbled, faltered, caused you so much distress.
But through it all, my heart's remained true,
Only you, my soulmate, my love, I pursue.
Like opposite electrons, we spin and collide,
Through multiverses, hand in hand we stride.
I've made some mistakes, my love, I admit,
Yet my love for you, unyielding, will never quit.

In the depths of my being I carry regret,
For the moments I failed you I cannot forget.
But know, my love, in every breath I take,
It's your love that sustains me, making me ache.
I apologise for the times I let you down,
For the tears that I caused - the upset, the frowns.
But amidst my imperfections and all of my flaws,
My love for you, unwavering, never withdraws.

Through the storms we've weathered, side by side,
You've been my anchor, my unwavering guide.
For you, my soulmate, I'd walk a thousand miles,
To heal your wounds, to bring back your smiles.
In the echoes of time, please hear my plea,
That my love for you will forever be.
I may not be perfect in anyone's view,
But my adoration of you is constant and true.

So let our love transcend the sky's expanse,
Like stars colliding in a celestial dance.
For you, my opposite electron, my soul's perfect mate,
I'll spend eternity making amends; that's my fate.
As in the vastness of the multiverses we roam,
I'll prove my love and rebuild what was known.
For I've never stopped loving you, my dear,
And I'll spend forever making that clear.

Is This Your Card?

From this deck of cards a world unfolds,
Where tales are spun and mysteries solved.
Tarot's ancient wisdom - a secret code,
Through a dance of symbols a story's bestowed.

The Fool steps forth with a carefree stride,
Embarking on a journey with nothing to hide.
With each card turned the future's appointed,
A tapestry of life, your fate is pinpointed.

The Magician wields power with a flick of the wrist,
Harnessing the elements; a sorcerer's twist.
With skill and charm he weaves his spell,
Unlocking secrets the cards alone tell.

The High Priestess is serene in her grace,
A guardian of secrets in a mystical space.
Guiding us through dreams in the depths of the mind,
A whisper of wisdom, a truth we might find.

The Emperor, a ruler so strong and proud,
With authority and order he stands unbowed.
A symbol of structure, of control and of might,
His presence commands a force to ignite.

The Lovers entwined is a tale of desire,
Two souls united, passion set afire.
Their hearts beat as one in love's tender embrace,
A divine connection, no challenge they'll face.

Cont'd

Is this Your Card?
(Cont'd..)

The Tower crumbles in a blaze of destruction,
Breaking illusions, causing chaos, disruption.
From the ashes, though, new beginnings arise, and
A chance to rebuild; see through much wiser eyes.

The Moon casts its glow - it's a beacon of dreams,
Revealing hidden truths, or so it seems.
Intuition's our guide navigating the night,
Unveiling mysteries, shadows taking flight.

The Sun shines bright, it's a symbol of joy,
Radiating a warmth no darkness can destroy.
With optimism and vitality it leads the way,
Illuminating paths for a brighter day.

The Wheel of Fortune spins destiny's dance,
Fortunes rise and fall in a cosmic trance.
With Fate's turning wheel we ride the tide,
Accepting life's changes with grace by our side.

So, let the cards speak and their tales unfold,
The language of symbols, a story to behold.
In the realm of tarot where wisdom resides,
Join the dance of Fate where your destiny hides.

Dartington

In a meadow where wildflowers grow,
Lived two pheasants running to and fro.
With feathers of vibrant hues they roamed,
A tapestry of colours in a natural home.

Close by, two humans, kind and gentle,
Befriended the birds and let them settle.
With hearts full of love and tender care,
Watching the family; they were always there.

In the golden dawn as the sun awoke,
The pheasants stretched their wings and spoke.
With graceful strides they explored the land,
Guided by the humans, their wings outfanned.

Through fields of green they would wander,
Under azure skies they'd sit and ponder.
The humans shared stories whispered and sung,
Creating a bond from which love sprung.

When storms brewed high and thunder roared,
The pheasants sought shelter, their fear outpoured.
The humans opened their doors with a wide smile,
Offering warmth and safety for a while.

Cont'd

Dartington
(Cont'd)

They nurtured the pheasants with tender care,
Feeding them seeds, their burdens to bear.
With gentle hands they turned fear around,
And with their love, sanctuary was found.

As seasons changed and time moved on,
The pheasant family grew, with young birds born.
The chicks spread wings with downy feathers,
And embarked on little adventures together.

And so, their bond grew ever stronger,
One neither side would ever squander.
In this tapestry of life where love transcends,
Lived those pheasants and their two dear friends.

For in the safety of nature's embrace,
Kindness and compassion find their place.
And in the hearts of humans and birds,
A friendship blossoms beyond any words.

Eights & Aces

In a smoky room where shadows played,
A man of chance his cards displayed,
A stranger sat with eyes so deep;
A wager made - a soul to keep.

Cards were dealt, prize placed on the bar…
An elixir from the fountain of Amrita.
With each card turned his heart would pound
Until the final call was found.

He'd won the game, he raised a cheer!
But in the stranger's gaze now fear,
For in his victory a curse was cast,
To walk the earth til all had passed.

The cities crumbled; forests died.
Where once whales sang, the oceans dried.
Humanity's last breath was drawn,
Yet he remained to greet the dawn.

In endless fields of dust and bone,
He walked the earth, always alone.
No voice to hear, no hand to hold,
Just memories of days grown cold.

The stars above his only friends
In this lonely walk that never ends.
A maddening silence, an empty space,
No living soul; no human trace.

He cursed the cards, the stranger's game.
The endless life, the timeless blame.
A wanderer in a world that death begot
In an echoing void that time forgot.

Symphonies in the Royal Forest

In the heart of the royal forest, a beekeeper resides.
His connection with the hive will never subside.
With gentle hands and care he tends to each bee,
A symphony of buzzing; a dance of unity.

The beekeeper, a guardian of nature's delicate thread,
In the royal forest, where wild flowers spread.
He listens to their whispers, their language unspoken,
A harmony of buzzing with respect that's unbroken.

In the royal forest they thrive as one,
A symbiotic connection under the sun.
Their dance of life, a testament to their connection,
A collaboration of nature, the hive's affection.

The beekeeper, a steward of this sacred place,
Protecting their home with unwavering grace.
In the royal forest their worlds intertwine,
A keeper and his hive have a bond divine.

Guardians

In the wild depths of the forest, where shadows
Dance their secret rituals,
Where the air carries stories like whispered spells,
There's a man; a witch; a soul - more than
Just flesh and bone.
He's stitched into the very essence of this place,
A living thread in its tapestry.
He strides among ancient sentinels, those trees.
Their bark the wrinkles of wisdom,
Leaves murmuring tales spun through aeons.
The earth's pulse beats beneath his feet,
A symphony of solitude,

And sunlight's brushstrokes painting love,
Longing in the air.
The ground's a mosaic of emerald whispers,
Air thick with pine
And earth's musky embrace is a reminder of life
Pulsing in every corner.
Each step is a dialogue with the heavy, peaty soil,
Each breath a communion with an ancient choir.
Foxes dart, rabbits play their silent
Games in the thicket,
While birds compose a freedom symphony,
Their wings slicing through sky.

Cont'd

Guardians
(Cont'd)

This is his orchestra; his wild symphony.
Life thriving in the quiet hum of existence;
A testament to untamed grace.
A river carves its path beneath watchful trees,
Waters cradling stories untold,
Secrets whispered in its flow.
He listens to its language:
Moss covered stones murmuring,
Pebbles conversing, shaped by the
Gentle waves of time.

As dusk cloaks the forest, transformation is ignited.
Under night's veil, they feel the rhythm shift.
The creatures of the dark awaken from their slumber,
An owl sings its wisdom to the night;
A deer finds cover in deep shadows.
In this nocturnal embrace he stands
Not just as a man
But as a guardian of the wild; a keeper of secrets.
He's woven into the fabric, the enchanted realm
Breathing life into it all.
He is part of something greater.
Something eternal.

Farewell

In the shires of Narnia, where magic thrives,
Lived a wise old man with a beard so grey,
Spending his days writing poetry and tales,
Of worlds where dreams and reality sway.
His name was known far and wide,
For his words held an enchanting grace.
With every verse, a story would unfold,
Taking readers to a mystical, wondrous place.

Beside him stood his loving wife, Nethiel,
A gentle soul with eyes sparkling bright.
Together they scribbled spells and sorcery,
Creating magic with every word they write.
In their cottage, nestled among the trees,
Two little dragons happily danced and played,
Their scales shimmered softly in vibrant hues,
In the enchanted land, they joyfully stayed.

The old man would sit by the fireplace,
His quill dancing on parchment with ease,
Words flowed from his heart and mind,
Capturing moments, emotions and mysteries.
He crafted landscapes with each new verse,
Breathing life into mythical creatures and lore.
His poetry whispered secrets of the universe,
Unfolding mystical tales never heard before.

                                              Cont'd

Farewell
(Cont'd)

The townsfolk would gather to hear his tales,
Mesmerised by the magick in his words,
He shared his knowledge and lessons of life,
As his voice soared like the songs of birds.
Through the years, his beard grew longer,
A testament to the wisdom he possessed;
A symbol of the countless stories he told
And the love and knowledge he expressed.

In the shires of Narnia the old man roamed,
With his loving wife and dragons by his side,
Their magic and poetry filling the air,
In this enchanting world they couldn't hide.
So let us cherish the wise old man,
With his beard so grey and his heart so true,
For his words and magic will forever live on,
In the tales he shared and the love he knew.

Not All Heroes Wear Tuxedos

In the quiet chaos of the city night,
Ollie, the tuxedo kitten, stood watch.
A guardian in the shadows,
Protecting Noodles, the baby tabby,
Fragile and small beneath the vastness of the sky.
His presence was a shield,
A silent vow of protection,
A flicker of hope against the cold and uncertainty,
Where every rustle in the dark
Could be a threat or a promise.

Noodles, trusting, found her courage
In the steadfastness of Ollie's gaze;
In the moments where silence spoke
Of loyalty, of companionship,
Of two souls intertwined in survival.
Then she came,
With hands that spoke of kindness,
Eyes that saw beyond the grime and fear,
A heart that opened worlds of warmth,
Transforming their cold nights into sunny mornings.

In her care, they found a haven.
A place where the shadows receded;
Where Noodles could unfurl into the softness of safety,
Where Ollie's vigilant, exhausted eyes
Could finally close.
In this new chapter, love wrapped around them
Like a gentle promise.
And Ollie's mission, once so urgent,
Became a story of courage and tenderness
Etched in the heart of the kindest lady they ever met.

Stand down, Ollie, your duty's done.

Reviews

People have said about Bob's poetry:

"Bob Christian's poetry demonstrates a versatile and thoughtful writing style. His work delves into a range of emotional and thematic territories, often with a personal and introspective touch. The poems are well-crafted, with vivid imagery and a strong sense of voice that engages the reader. Bob Christian's poetry is a compelling exploration of the human experience."

"Bob Christian's poetry is a captivating exploration of the duality of the human experience, weaving together threads of darkness and light, challenge and comfort. His words possess a raw, visceral quality that cuts straight to the heart, inviting the reader on a journey through the shadowy recesses of the psyche and the radiant landscapes of the soul."

Printed in Great Britain
by Amazon